MĀORI RAFTER & TĀNIKO DESIGNS

SELECTED BOOKS BY W.J. PHILLIPPS

Maori Carving, Harry H. Tombs, Wellington, 1938
The Fishes of New Zealand, Thomas Avery and Sons, New Plymouth, 1940
Maori Design, Harry H. Tombs, Wellington, 1943
Maori Art, Harry H. Tombs, Wellington, 1946
Maori Houses and Food Stores, Government Printer, Wellington, 1952
Maori Life and Custom, A.H. & A.W. Reed, Wellington, 1966

MĀORI RAFTER & TĀNIKO DESIGNS

W.J. PHILLIPPS

Published by Oratia Books, Oratia Media Ltd, 783 West Coast Road, Oratia, Auckland 0604, New Zealand (www.oratia.co.nz).

Originally published in 1943 as *Māori Designs*
This edition copyright © 2025 Oratia Books

The copyright holders assert their moral rights in the work.

This book is copyright. Except for the purposes of fair reviewing, no part of this publication may be reproduced or transmitted in any form or by any means, whether electronic, digital or mechanical, including photocopying, recording, any digital or computerised format, or any information storage and retrieval system, including by any means via the Internet, without permission in writing from the publisher. Infringers of copyright render themselves liable to prosecution.

ISBN 978-1-99-004279-9

Editors: Carolyn Lagahetau, Erena Shingade
Designer: Sarah Elworthy

Acknowledgement is made to Sylvia S. Baker and Margaret A. Morison for preparation of the images on pages 44–55, and to Tony Murdoch, Smith's Bookshop, Christchurch for referral to the 1960 edition.

First published 1943 by Harry H. Tombs Limited at the Wingfield Press, Wellington.
Second edition 1945
Third edition 1960
This edition 2025

Printed in China

CONTENTS

About the author   7
Introduction to the 1960 edition   9

RAFTER DESIGNS   13
    He koru   14
    He whakairo tuhituhi   21

TĀNIKO DESIGNS   41
    Tāniko designs   42

TUKUTUKU DESIGNS   61
    A note on decorative panels   62

Glossary   68
Bibliography   71

ABOUT THE AUTHOR

William John (W.J.) Phillipps was born in Oamaru in 1893. In 1915, he joined the staff of the Dominion Museum (now Te Papa Tongarewa), Wellington, where he worked as an ethnologist, ichthyologist, ornithologist and scientific illustrator. During a career that spanned five decades, he published about 200 scientific papers and authored several books in the fields of zoology and anthropology. He passed away in 1967.

Out from the past there is bequeathed to us a heritage — an art of abiding beauty peculiarly our own — a system of design that once dwelt not on paper or parchment but in the mentality of a great people. It is for us today to see to it that in our national life all that is best in Māori art will be revivified to live again in a new and better age.

W.J. PHILLIPPS, 1960

Art by Augustus Hamilton, 1897. Of these, 17 have been selected, and are here included by courtesy of the Council of the Royal Society of New Zealand, the publishers of the above-mentioned work. In the art productions of elements of design, I have had the assistance of Miss E. Borthwick, formerly Art Teacher, Feilding Agricultural High School.

Mr C.R.H. Taylor, Librarian, Turnbull Library, gave permission to use odd notes from the manuscript by Ven. Archdeacon H.W. Williams, dated 24th June 1914, and made to accompany his original sketches now in that institution. To the above my grateful thanks are due. I have also to place on record my appreciation of helpful discussions with Mr J.M. McEwen, at present Assistant Secretary, Department of Island Territories. In regard to the section dealing with tāniko, I have also to acknowledge with thanks the help of Miss Sylvia S. Baker.

W. J. Phillipps.

PUBLISHER'S NOTE: papers and books referred to in the text are all listed in the Bibliography, p. 71.

INTRODUCTION TO THE 1960 EDITION

Throughout New Zealand is an ever-growing band, Māori and Pākehā, whose minds turn with interest to the unknown in the arts and crafts of ancient Māoridom. The general interest that has attended the publication of my small book *Māori Carving* leads me strongly to the conviction that in our educational and national life there is a place that Māori art alone can fill, for is not this the inalienable right of our children? The adaptation of all that is best and finest to meet the artistic requirements of a coming era, and the understanding of the elaborate systems of design built up by generations of craftsmen, should now be our first duty.

In these few pages it is my intention to do something, as far as I am aware, not previously attempted, and that is to analyse Māori rafter patterns and discuss their component parts in such a manner that a clearer understanding and a greater appreciation of them will be the result. I write from the basis of the student rather than from that of the advanced critic, remembering always that in conservative simplicity these patterns were born, and in that same simplicity must their beauty be interpreted.

In their original series, some 29 designs were portrayed in *Māori*

RAFTER DESIGNS

HE KORU

We introduce the study of rafter design with a consideration of an important element, which gives us the key to much that is involved in the study of both design and carving. I refer to the koru, a simple curving stalk with a bulb at one end. As a painted design in the rafter patterns the koru reaches its highest expression. We are not here concerned with the origin of the koru except to note that it appears in nature in the curving frond of the tree fern, when it is usually called pikopiko or pītau. When painted for use in rafter patterns the koru is essentially a single spiral, but when painted or carved in outline, as in an illustration, various types of double spiral may arise.

In order to understand the relationship of the koru to Māori spirals I have compiled a series of diagrams (Figures 1 to 3, opposite) to illustrate how the koru design carved in outline may have given rise to various spiral conceptions. Actually, it will be noticed that three classes of spirals are portrayed, and you will recognise that these three types contain within themselves the integral features of all main types of Māori spiral. The first two (Figures 1 and 2) may be classified as 'simple', and the third (Figure 3) as 'compound'.

The possible development of the S-curve spiral from the koru is more self-evident than is the development of the simple

FIGURES 1, 2, 3 The koru and the double spiral, possible lines of relationship.

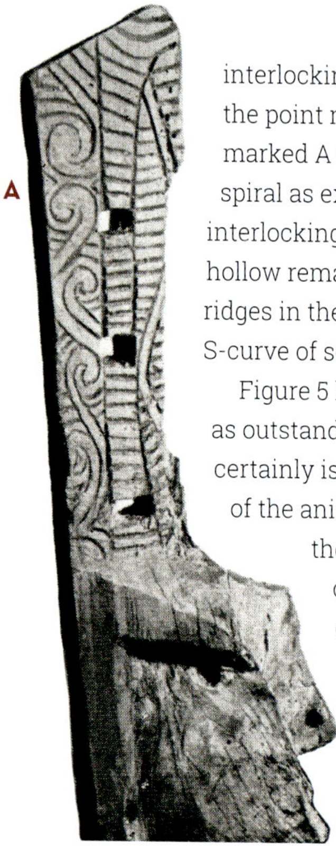

interlocking spiral as seen in Figure 2. In Figure 4 at the point marked A, and in Figure 6 at the point also marked A we have an intermediate stage of the koru spiral as exemplified in the drawings (Figure 1C). The interlocking spiral is often only partially closed, enough hollow remaining between the commencement of the ridges in the centre to enable the student to trace an S-curve of some sort.

Figure 5 has been described by Dr H.D. Skinner as outstanding, and for purposes of our study it certainly is unique. Most of the design on the body of the animal seems to be founded on the koru. From the secondary carved ornament on this chest it would also be a simple matter to prove that the S-curve spiral developed from a bending line. On this figure, in the centre, near the point marked B, we have a koru design broken in the middle, as illustrated in Figure 2. On old burial chests the interlocking spiral is not so common as the S-curve type.

There appears to be little doubt that the compound spirals as evidenced by Figures 7 and 8 are the modern development of much simpler types.

In the series illustrated by Figure 3 I have attempted to show one of the methods by which a compound spiral may be evolved. Compare the outline of the compound spiral of Figure 3 with the photograph as seen in Figure 8. In this latter spiral the S-curve is notched, this being a feature of many Whanganui and Taranaki spirals, but at Rotorua (whenever this compound type is

FIGURE 4 A very old stone-carved canoe sternpost.
T.W. DOWNES, WHANGANUI MUSEUM

FIGURE 5 Old stone-carved burial chest.
AUCKLAND MUSEUM

used) we find a majority of spirals with S-curve plain ridges in the centre.

As all carvers are aware, it is impossible to carve the S-curve groove without becoming conscious of the resulting partial interlock of the ridges. The deeper and wider the S-curve is cut, the narrower and steeper do the partially interlocking ridges become (Figure 6, B). It is a very short development for the carver to interlock the ridges or to place a row of chevrons or crescents thereon and so produce more attractive types of spirals. To get the true interlock we have only to omit the S-curve. We have seen how easily the partially interlocking spiral could be developed from the S-curve type. To me it appears unlikely that the converse would be true.

Some old koru designs are found engraved on the walls of South Canterbury caves in the limestone district about Albury and the Ōpihi River. Careful examination of this series would seem to demonstrate that these old-time South Island Māori were acquainted with the S-curve design founded on or associated with the koru.

FIGURE 6 Diminutive burial chest.
DOMINION MUSEUM

The idea of a central rod dividing into two branching koru is found here, as in the North Island, where it has been used to symbolise the hammerhead shark with an eye on the end of a protrusion on each side of the head.

No consideration of the koru in Māori art would be complete without some mention of its use in the adorning of the ipu whakairo, or carved gourd vessel. Gourd vessels are largely used for holding and carrying food or water, those that were the property of chiefs or important personages being usually covered with designs founded on the koru. Such few

FIGURE 7 Compound interlocking spiral.
GISBORNE DISTRICT, J.T. SALMON

FIGURE 8 Compound spiral.
DOMINION MUSEUM CARVING FROM THE WHANGANUI RIVER, J.T. SALMON

ipu whakairo as remain in our museums illustrate patterns likely to be traditional, for they would have been done under the eyes of the old tohunga. A large example in the Dominion Museum (now Museum of New Zealand Te Papa Tongarewa) illustrates the use of diagonal and oblique lines dividing outside areas of the ipu into symmetrical areas nicely filled with koru designs.

In an example from Lake Rotoaira we find groups of koru taking the form of independent elements not connected with any main stem. Many bulbs are larger than usual, but this is a feature of some Lake Taupō-area rafter patterns.

A very old gourd vessel in the museum collection was presented by the late A.H. Turnbull. A large oval uncarved area marks the resting-point below the vessel. Halfway between the margin of this oval area and the upper edge a circular band runs round the ipu, koru designs emanating from it above and below. Two features stand out, assigning to this ipu an important position in the history of Māori design. These are, firstly, a number of small circular areas used to give greater effect to the koru; and, secondly, bands of carved plaiting or basketry. The circular areas are not necessarily degenerate spirals but may be bulbs of the koru devoid of their stalks.

That no attempted basic classification of the simple Māori spiral types has hitherto been discussed appears to be due to the prominence usually given to the interlocking spiral and its instant appeal to the European mind. Professor J. Macmillan Brown, in his work entitled *Maori and Polynesian* came nearest to the realisation of an S-curve basis as a possible origin for all spirals when he suggested that Māori spirals were copied from the coiling rope. One student (the late Grant Taylor) has drawn my attention to the fact that in Māori canoes, mooring ropes are always rolled in a double fashion, and not single, as on English ships.

The old type of tattoo figured by Cook and copied in Figure 9 is simply a Māori rafter pattern applied to the face, the koru being turned into S-curve spirals and the fine lines remaining as an adornment. It is reasonable to assume that, in the history of a race, painted design would precede carving. Accordingly, we should find in rafter patterns and tattoo an element of design that we can relate to early carving, and this is present in the koru.

George Graham, in the *Journal of the Polynesian Society*, quotes some legends of Maraetai, Auckland, as narrated by Anaru Makiwhara of Ngāi Tai. The following quotation is of much interest here:

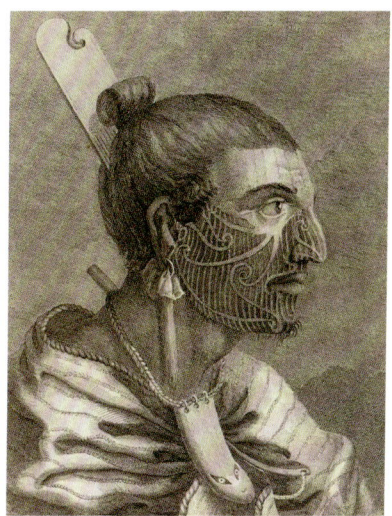

FIGURE 9 Tattooed chief as figured in Cook's voyages.
J.T. SALMON

> On the foreshore to the east of Howick grows a large pohutukawa tree known still by Ngati-tai as Te Tuhi-a-Manawatere. This man, Manawatere, came from Hawaiki; he did not come in a canoe; he glided over the ripples of the waves. He came by way of Hauraki to Marae-tai (enclosed sea). He landed at this pohutukawa, and made his mark (tuhi) thereon; using a kind of red ochre paint known as karamea. The mark he made was thus
>
>
>
> and was a sign to those following that he had come that way. Hence a Ngati-tai proverb in respect of things or persons lost and being searched for among us: Ma te tuhi rapa a Manawatere ke kitea — 'By the vivid mark of Manawatere it will be found.'

Here we have the S-curve known as a design in those far-off days of early Polynesian migration — so far off, apparently, as to have become legendary. If the tradition can be relied on, did the S-curve come first into Māori carving and have the early burial chest S-curves any relationship to the vivid mark of Manawatere? Who shall now say? But it may be so.

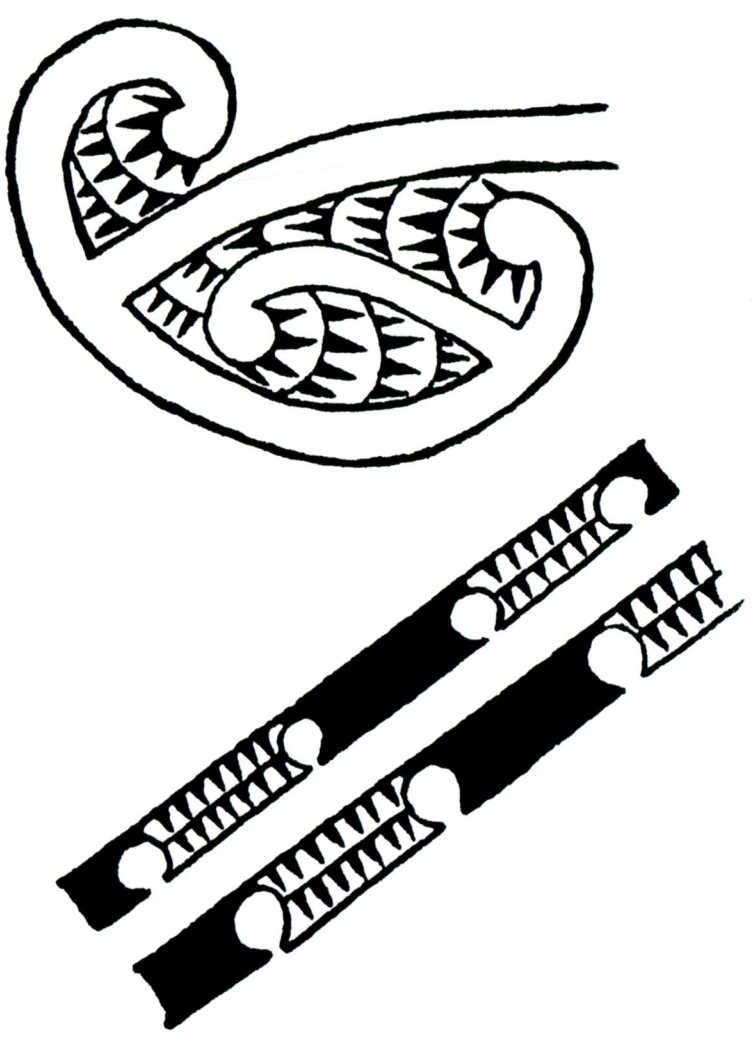

FIGURE 10 This sketch illustrates the use of 'embattlement' lines with small triangles attached. Note the resemblance to tāniko. This is a rather rare form of decoration which has disappeared under the influences of modern carving technique.
MAORI ART BY AUGUSTUS HAMILTON, PLATE 13 – POROURANGI CARVED HOUSE, EAST COAST

HE WHAKAIRO TUHITUHI

From Augustus Hamilton's book *Māori Art*, we give the following extract as written by the Rev. H.W. Williams:

> Any scientific discussion of that branch of Maori art which comprised the decoration of the whare by painting is rendered extremely difficult, if not impossible, by the fact that none of the old school of painters are now living, and little if any of their work has survived them.
>
> The Maori decorator does not copy; that is to say, he does not draw from a pattern, but carries the design as far as may be in his head. To transfer the design to the material before him, he apparently forms a mental projection of it upon his board and traces the outline, working in the colour afterwards. It may be dangerous to argue from the habits observed now back to the custom of the ancient tohunga; but certainly this method of producing a pattern does not at all accord with European notions. Instead of laying down the main elements of the pattern and working in the details later, some, at any rate, of the modern painters work as stated above, and the method produces certain results of which traces

> appear in drawings made some years ago. For instance, in an outline sketch of a pattern made by a Maori for the writer, the bulk of the drawing was correctly done; but in one place two elements of the projection evidently had undergone mental displacement; and there was nothing for it but to draw them where they could be got in. If colour could have been filled in a new pattern would have been produced. Analogous to this is the defect which may be seen in almost any Maori whare — of patterns drawn too large for the slab. Instead of cramping the pattern to suit the material, the artist draws what he can and omits the rest …
>
> The pigments used in these decorations were mainly soot and red ochre (kokowai), the white being the self-coloured timber; but it is said that the Ngati-porou in the Waiapu district sometimes added a blue-grey, produced by a slimy clay known as tutae-whetu. The colours were arranged to the taste of the artist; as a rule, rather avoiding a set formation … In the better paintings the colour was not laid on flat but in finely-embattled lines which followed the main curves of the pattern …

In regard to the naming of these designs there appears to be ample proof of the statement already made by Sir Peter Buck (Te Rangi Hīroa) that the Māori evolved their designs first and applied the names afterwards, using simple parallels in their environment. This will be obvious to the student who examines these pages with care. Elsdon Best was in agreement with the Rev. Mr Williams that horizontal lines and sometimes vertical lines appearing in given designs were innovations of modern times — that basically in his rafter patterns the Māori artisan much preferred curving lines. Whether in pre-European times this custom was rigidly observed we cannot now say.

However, inside the body of Māori art is another and unrelated series of designs that in some degree may have influenced the curvilinear rafter patterns. These are the tāniko designs, rectilinear types that appear to have evolved from types easily applicable to the woven fabrics, so the statement that 'in considering ornament the ancient tohunga hated straight lines' seems hardly correct.

In any study of rafter patterns, the first consideration must always be the foundations on which they have been built, so the first plate is supplied to illustrate the separate elements in the patterns. These form the basis of our study and one by one should be memorised so that they can be drawn at will as required. Only then can one hope to memorise the more complicated and completed designs that follow. In presenting these elements of design only essential features are included. Thus clarity of visual imagery is assured, making them practically self-explanatory when compared with the remaining series.

FIGURE 11 (PAGES 24–25)

Here, the first row of designs, A and B, illustrate the main forms that the koru assumes in design, while C, D, E and F portray what we may term the umbrella pattern, the umbrella being formed by two koru in C, D, and E, with a more evolved umbrella pattern in F. G, H, and I illustrate the branching koru and the manner in which it may very readily give rise to the complicated double spiral founded on an S-curve (see D).

L illustrates the S-curve spiral with arms of red and black partially interlocking, while M shows how the curious design there portrayed is built up. Two half-crescents are taken and joined above, and two koru bulbs are hollowed out from each to give an artistic effect. N apparently is built up of a crescent above and two koru below, as the dotted lines show. An unusual koru type appears in O and P, and a striking background effect is the result.
In O is a koru with a bulb at each end, and in P the koru outlines are separated to enclose an area that takes on a somewhat crescent shape.

Q also illustrates tāniko patterns. These are copied from a work by George French Angas entitled *The New Zealanders Illustrated* and from Hamilton's *Māori Art*. The main basic element of the tāniko is the equilateral triangle, which automatically originates from the zigzag line. Diamonds are, of course, double triangles. It is in the remarkable methods of alternate colouring that the artistic effect is

FIGURE 11

A B C D E F

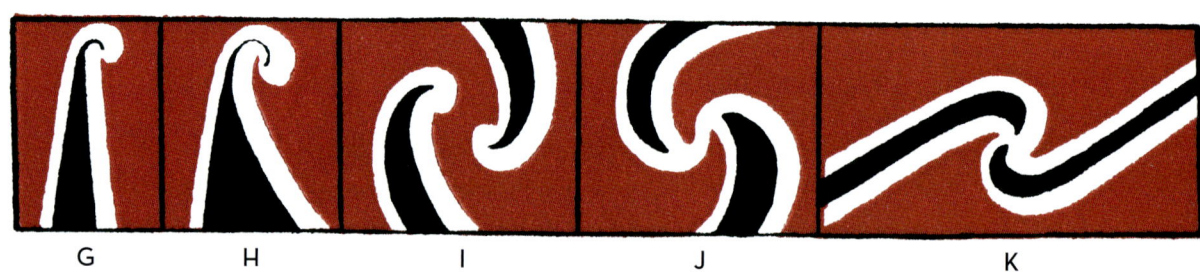

G H I J K

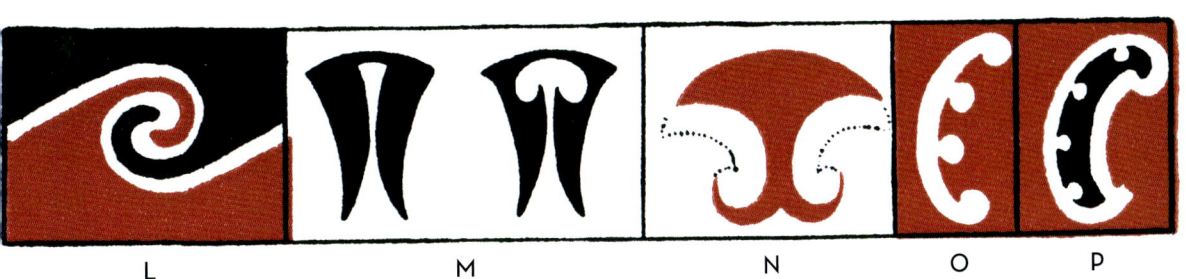

L M N O P

Q

achieved. Tāniko was used as a rafter design only on the heke tipi, a board placed above the poupou at the base of the rafters.

FIGURE 12 (PAGES 28–29)

In A we have basically a comparatively wide zigzag line dividing the given area into a series of isosceles triangles with obtuse angles above or below. From the centre of each straight line a koru runs toward the right through the triangular area. Another koru originating near the bulb of the last-mentioned folds in an elongate S-curve to fill the space opposite the obtuse angle. This folding has also been described as the reversed curve. In the original series this design was copied from a photograph of a similar design from Tūhoe country.

In B and the previous design, A, the Rev. Mr Williams sees the pointed flower of the kākā beak, kōwhai ngutu kākā (*Clianthus puniceus*), the main design obviously appearing inside the outer curves of the elongate S-curve koru. In considering B we notice that the central horizontal line and a series of vertical lines divide the area into rectangular areas inside which two koru are extended in circular fashion with ends coalesced and bulbs above and below the centre line. As in A the elongate S-curve koru arises near the bulbs. Here also we meet the 'balanced koru' — that is, an upright stalk with an umbrella pattern bending down (or up) with terminal bulbs — two koru swung around on the end of a stalk. This design was also included from a photograph from Tūhoe country.

C illustrates a well-known East Coast and Arawa design, which the Rev. Mr Williams states is 'said to be a conventionalized patiki or flat-fish'. The design is seen in the diamond shape enclosed by the two undulating lines running along the rafter length. Koru placed in pairs fill all spaces with precision. At this point we may mention that almost invariably the koru is swung around in such a manner that in two, or, rarely three places it nearly touches its related elements. Originally, this drawing was executed from a house at Muriwai, Tūranganui-a-Kiwa/Poverty Bay.

The design shown in D is remarkable in that the above-mentioned principle of 'balanced koru' has been applied on a considerable scale. The straight vertical line is an important feature ending above or below in two long umbrella arms running downwards or upwards to support a leaf-like structure, which in its outer construction is similar to the circular design of B. The inner construction of the leaf structure consists of two pairs of koru, large and small. The common native orchid, *Coryanthes*, has leaves very similar to the type here seen. In the Turnbull Library manuscript this is described as an Arawa form of mangōpare.

FIGURE 13 (PAGES 30–31)

This design has an affinity with B and D of Figure 12, in that the essential features consist of a circular or oval form built up of two koru with bulbs facing. Here the leaf-like design is at the end of a stalk as in Figure 12D, but this stalk is undulatory, swinging alternately upwards and downwards to join into the top of the leaf shape. The Rev. Mr Williams tells us that this design is known as ngutukura, a pattern once very popular in Tūranganui-a-Kiwa/Poverty Bay.

Drawn around an undulatory line of perfect symmetry and balanced on a central curving stalk, the well-known design shown in Figure 13B illustrates the use of the umbrella pattern combined with the koru. The true 'balanced koru' feature appears only in the smallest pair of koru present. Apparently this design is the one that more than any other is said to symbolise the hammerhead shark, which has its eyes on projections from the head. This, however, has little resemblance to the pattern. I suggest that, originally, the balanced koru suggested the association. The original pattern was copied from the tāhuhu of a house erected at Kaiti, Gisborne, about the year 1849.

The Rev. Mr Williams states that the design illustrated in C is supposed to represent the waves of the sea and that originally it had no mid-rib. If we omit the mid-rib and take the white designs as the pattern we notice how they roll at intervals in a folding S-curve, the basis of many Māori double-spiral designs. The S-curve prevents the interlock of red and white. Pairs of koru with origins not directly opposite branch off at intervals. Here again is another perfectly good theory as to how the double spiral originated. A line folds in continuous rhythm and the double spiral appears. This is yet another design originally copied from photographs from Tūhoe country.

FIGURE 12

A

B

C

D

FIGURE 13

A

B

C

D

In Figure 13D, the koru appears in two forms, (1) the simple small and secondary elements of decoration, and (2) a large branching folded type illustrating with perfection its evolution into an S-curve. Let the student study one of these curved koru and see how ingeniously the inner edge of the koru runs into the S-curve hollows. This design is copied from a house at Pakowai, near Waerenga-a-Hika, Tūranganui-a-Kiwa/Poverty Bay.

FIGURE 14 (OPPOSITE)

Comparing Figure 13D with Figure 14A, we notice that there is an essential similarity between them in that the S-curve is present as a central feature and lines run into the hollows. There is no circle in Māori art save the type here seen, and I take the circles around which white and black are constructed to be bulbs of koru that have lost their stalks. Allowing the vision to see only black and red patterns, we see how four elongate elements of design arise from the centre of a spiral. The Rev. Mr Williams, in the manuscript preserved in the Turnbull Library, calls this pattern 'Maui'. The hook of Maui is to be seen in the partially interlocking coloured patterns. These patterns are designed by Tamati Ngakaho, the decorator of Rāpata Wahawaha's famous house at Waiomatatini (Porourangi), on the Waiapu River.

Rev. Mr Williams tells us that Figure 14B represents one of the patterns called puhoro, correctly represented only in black and white. In view of the preceding remarks on koru we will see that essentially it is a form of dividing koru. It is a difficult design to draw. The centre points of the koru bulbs must be plotted first and the white lines carefully followed. This pattern is placed under the bows of war canoes — perhaps to symbolise speed, the curling waves and the forward-moving canoe.

C illustrates a pattern similar to the former and also called puhoro, but it is on a larger scale and illustrates well how the koru bulb gives rise to partially interlocking black and red lines of the double spiral. The term puhoro also refers to tattoo marks on the thigh or arm, and these appear to be related to this design. Both this pattern and the former are copied from Arawa originals.

FIGURE 14

A

B

C

FIGURE 15 (PAGES 36–37)

Figure 15A shows one of the designs called by Rev. Mr Williams ngutu kākā, literally, the lip (or beak) of the kākā parrot, which the pointed ends of the crescent might well symbolise. Crescent shapes alternate in position, the horns pointing to the centre of the inner curves of the crescents above or below. The circular koru bulbs encroaching on the crescent shape add much to its charm and beauty. Because of the importance of the moon in its relation to the daily activities of ancient Māori life, I have no hesitation in associating this design with the crescent, whatever its later appellation may have been.

In B the crescent shapes are arranged to fill a more or less circular space, the horns of the inner ones almost joining to enclose a central oval. Here, as in all this group, there is no doubt that the coloured crescents form the design as well as any subsidiary shapes that may appear. The number of koru bulbs increases to three on small crescents and four on large.

As with A, the design shown in C is called ngutu kākā by Rev. Mr Williams. Crescents interlock there as also here, but a new feature makes its appearance, fitting into the hollow of the crescent. The pointed ends of this element might easily be comparable to beaks of kākā. We notice here, as in practically all rafter patterns, that there is no beginning and no end to them. The rhythm is continuous and at the ends of the given space, elements of the pattern are incomplete.

Simplicity and elegance appear side by side in D. The smallest schoolchild could appreciate the beauty in its balanced features. In the hollow of crescents is another new design. This also appears to be founded on the koru, for, as already noted, the sides are in the shape of koru lying on their backs. The small edge design is also closely related. All drawings in Figure 15 were made by an old Māori, Pakerau, of Waipiro Bay.

FIGURE 16 (PAGES 38–39)

The Rev. Mr Williams states that the design illustrated in A is said to be called pītau a Manaia. Pītau is the name given to the opening frond of the tree fern, while manaia is the bird-headed man, a side-face figure of Māori carving art. Regarding the white as the design, we notice koru with bulbs at each end as well as along their length. The folding spiral also is present, as well as another figure that appears also in the old, restored patterns of the Tūranga House. From evidence received from Māori living at Tūranganui-a-Kiwa/Poverty Bay, Mr Harold Hamilton regarded this as the ngū, or squid, a small example of which appears to the left of the lower centre. This design was originally copied from the maihi of Te Poho o Rāwiri, a house erected at Gisborne, about the year 1849.

Another feature also common in the Tūranga House is seen in B. This is the long crescent-like shape completely surrounded with what may be double koru devoid of bulbs at the end. Wide undulating clear spaces also probably symbolise squid or octopus, although a variation of this design is said to be called kape rua. The Rev. Mr Williams states that puhoro also is applied to this pattern. This design was copied from Te Poho o Rāwiri.

FIGURE 15

A

B

C

D

FIGURE 16

A

B

FIGURE 27 Kaitaka cloak.
AUCKLAND MUSEUM

TUKUTUKU DESIGNS

A NOTE ON DECORATIVE PANELS

Māori decorative house panels, tukutuku, fill the spaces between the wall slabs of rectangular houses. The wall slabs, termed poupou, are sometimes carved, their main function being to support the lower ends of the rafters. The panel space between the poupou is termed moana. The panel itself is made by binding together a series of vertical flower stalks (kākaho) of the toetoe with horizontal rods of a common fern, or laths of tōtara manufactured to suit. The rods or laths are termed kaho tara by Te Arawa and kaho tarai on the East Coast. In very modern houses fluted boards have been used to simulate tukutuku.

It was in the manner of stitching or tying together these elements that the designs of the tukutuku panels were achieved. In modern times all work is done with the fingers, but formerly a wooden needle-like implement was used. For small panels one worker formerly did the lot, with the panel suspended horizontally, but in larger houses two workers were required, one working on each side, the stakes and rods being held in position on a frame especially made for the purpose. A cross-stitch was the one first taught. This was known as pūkanohi aua (herrings' eyes) on the

FIGURE 28 Poupou from the carved house Te Hau-ki-Tūranga before its re-erection in the new Dominion Museum building in 1936.
J.T. SALMON

FIGURE 29 Tukutuku workers for Dominion Museum carved house, Te Hau-ki-Tūranga, about 1935. Carver Thomas Heberley (Te Ātiawa) on right, author W.J. Phillipps on left, back row.
EVENING POST

FIGURE 30 Tukutuku panels from Te Hau-ki-Tūranga, left to right: (1) Purapura whetū, star dust, or roimata, tears. (2) Kaokao, armpit, or niho taniwha, dragon's teeth. (3) Waharua or waharua kopito, usually the former, double-mouth. (4) Pātikitiki, the common diamond shaped flounder. (5) Roimata toroa, albatross tears. (6) Poutama, step design.
J.T. SALMON

4

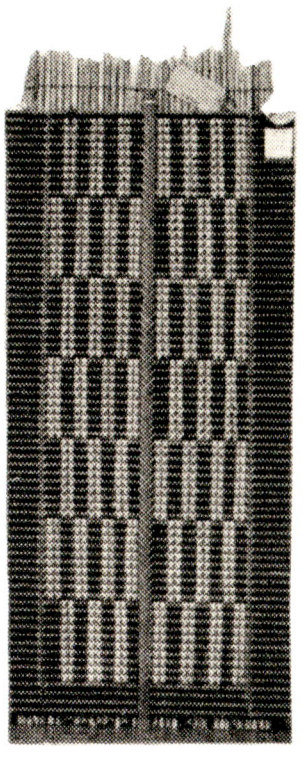

5

6

East Coast. Purapura whetū (star seeds) is the East Coast name. Names as supplied in the accompanying figure are beautifully fanciful. The design came first and then the name. For example, the young albatrosses are said to weep as the fowlers approach, knowing their fate, so we have the name in a tukutuku design: roimata toroa, albatross tears.

FIGURE 31 Te Hau-ki-Tūranga, the oldest whare whakairo in existence, pictured at Te Papa Tongarewa, Wellington, in 2009. Raharuhi Rukupō of Rongowhakaata led its construction in the 1840s using steel tools, and it reflects early Pākehā influence in its design.
111 EMERGENCY, WIKIMEDIA COMMONS

GLOSSARY

AONUI
pattern of triangles used in tāniko design

ARAMOANA
zigzag pattern used in tāniko design

HEKE TIPI
board placed above the poupou in a house or meeting house

HĪNAU
tall forest tree with long leaves, white flowers and edible berries

IPU
vessel made from a gourd

IPU WHAKAIRO
carved vessel made from a gourd

KAHO TARA
rods or laths used in making tukutuku panels

KAITAKA
flax-fibre cloak with a tāniko border

KĀKĀ
native parrot with feathers of brown, green and red

KĀKAHO
stalk of the toetoe, often used for lining the walls of buildings

KĀKAHU
clothing

KAOKAO
armpit, a chevron pattern used in tukutuku panels

KAPE RUA
type of kōwhaiwhai pattern

KARAMEA
red ochre

KŌKŌWAI
red ochre

KORU
fold, loop, coil or single spiral

KŌWHAI
various species of native tree with yellow flowers

KŌWHAI NGUTU KĀKĀ
native tree with bright red flowers, also known as kākā beak

KŌWHAIWHAI
ornamentation used on the rafters of meeting houses

MAIHI
barge boards of a meeting house decorated with carving or ornamentation

MANAIA
stylised figure said to represent a spiritual messenger

MANGŌPARE
hammerhead shark

MAUI
hero of Polynesian mythology

MOANA
panel space between the poupou in a house

NGŪ
type of marine animal, usually octopus or squid

NGUTU KĀKĀ
beak of the kākā parrot

NGUTUKURA
type of kōwhaiwhai pattern

NIHO
tooth or tooth-shaped design

NIHO KATA
incisors (*lit.* laughing teeth)

NIHO PŪ
pre-molar or molar teeth

NIHO TANIWHA
dragon's teeth, a pattern used in tukutuku and tāniko design

PAHEKE
double or single lines separating triangles in a pattern

PARAWAI
cloak made of flax fibre

PĀTIKI
flounder or flatfish, a design symbolising a source of food

PĀTIKITIKI
diamond-shaped flounder, a pattern used in tukutuku design

PIKOPIKO
curving frond of a tree fern

PĪTAU
curving frond of a tree fern, a type of spiral design

PĪTAU A MANAIA
kōwhaiwhai design featuring a double spiral

PŌHUTUKAWA
native tree with red flowers that bloom in December

POUPOU
upright slabs in a house or meeting house

POUTAMA
step design used in tukutuku panels

PUHORO
type of kōwhaiwhai pattern

PŪKANOHI AUA
herrings' eyes, a pattern used in tukutuku design. See also purapura whetū

PŪKEKO
swamp hen

PURAPURA WHETŪ
star seeds, a pattern used in tukutuku design. See also pūkanohi aua

ROIMATA
tears

ROIMATA TOROA
albatross tears, a pattern used in tukutuku design

TĀHUHU
ridgepole of a house or meeting house

TĀNEKAHA
celery pine, used for dying flax fibre

TĀNIKO
type of weaving

TOETOE
native plant used for tukutuku panels

TOHUNGA
priest, healer, expert

TŌTARA
large forest tree

TUHI
mark, writing

TUKEMATA
zigzag pattern with serrated lines used in tāniko design

TUKUTUKU
decorative house panels

TŪTAE-WHETŪ
star droppings, blue-grey clay

WAEWAE PŪKEKO
feet of the pūkeko, a pattern used in tāniko design

WAHARUA
double-mouth, a pattern used in tukutuku design

WHAKANIHO
serrated or toothed pattern

WHAKARUA KOPITO
pattern with lozenge-shaped units

WHARE
house

BIBLIOGRAPHY

Angas, George French, *The New Zealanders Illustrated*. Thomas McLean, London, 1847.

Buck, Sir Peter (Te Rangi Hīroa), 'On the Maori art of weaving cloaks, capes and kilts' in *Dominion Museum Bulletin*, no. 3, 1911, pp. 69–90.

—, *The Evolution of Maori Clothing*. Memoirs of the Polynesian Society, vol. 7, Board of Maori Ethnological Research, New Plymouth, 1926.

Graham, George, 'Te Tuhi-a-Manawatere and Other Legends of Marae-tai, Auckland' in *Journal of the Polynesian Society*, vol. 30, no. 120, 1921, pp. 252–53.

Hamilton, Augustus, *The Art Workmanship of the Maori Race in New Zealand*. New Zealand Institute, Dunedin, 1896.

—, *Transactions and Proceedings of the New Zealand Institute*, vol. 30, 1897.

—, *Maori Art*. New Zealand Institute, Wellington, 1897. Republished by Holland Press, London, 1977.

Macmillan Brown, John, *Maori and Polynesian: Their Origin, History and Culture*. Hutchinson & Co., London, 1907. Republished by AMS Press, New York, 1977.

Mead, Hirini Moko, *Taniko Weaving*. A.H & A.W. Reed, Wellington, 1952. Revised and republished as *Te Whatu Tāniko*. Oratia Books, Auckland, 2019.

Phillipps, W.J., 'A review of the elasmobranch fishes of New Zealand: No. 1' in *New Zealand Journal of Science and Technology*, vol. 6, 1924, pp. 257–69.

—, *Maori Carving*. Harry H. Tombs, Wellington, 1938. Revised and republished as *Maori Carving Illustrated*. Reed, Wellington, 1997.

Williams, Herbert William (H.W.), *Notes on Maori Rafter Patterns*. Unpublished manuscript. National Library records show that these notes accompany the drawings of Māori rafter patterns by Williams collected and reproduced in Augustus Hamilton's *The Art Workmanship of the Maori Race in New Zealand*. New Zealand Institute, Dunedin, 1896.

FURTHER READING

Brown, Deidre S., 'Te Hau ki Turanga' in *Journal of the Polynesian Society*, vol. 105, no. 1, 1996, pp. 7–26.

Graham, Brett, 'Whakairo — Māori carving — Carving, 19th century' in Te Ara, the Encyclopedia of New Zealand, 22 Oct 2014, www.TeAra.govt.nz/en/interactive/43104/te-hau-ki-turanga-meeting-house

Metekingi, Bronte, 'Future of stolen wharenui up for discussion as Te Papa exhibition closes' in Stuff, 7 May 2022, www.stuff.co.nz/pou-tiaki/128464831/future-of-stolen-wharenui-up-for-discussion-as-te-papa-exhibition-closes

OTHER MĀORI ARTS AND CRAFTS RESOURCES FROM ORATIA BOOKS

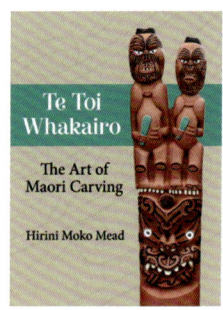

TE TOI WHAKAIRO: THE ART OF MAORI CARVING
Hirini Moko Mead

978-0-947506-37-7
PB, 242 x 182 mm portrait, 276 pp, b&w

Beginning with carving's mythical origins, *Te Toi Whakairo* explores the evolution of styles and techniques through the four main artistic periods to the present day. It provides detailed explanations of carving styles in different parts of Aotearoa using examples from meeting houses and leading artists, and gives practical guidance for use of materials, tools, techniques, surface and background decoration, the human figure, and carving poupou.

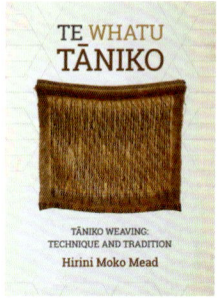

TE WHATU TĀNIKO: TĀNIKO WEAVING — TECHNIQUE AND TRADITION
Hirini Moko Mead

978-0-947506-61-2
PB, 250 x 185 mm portrait, 136 pp, b&w

Weaving and dyeing the fibres of native flax creates beautiful patterns that are used to adorn clothing, with distinctive styles that have evolved over centuries of creativity. *Te Whatu Tāniko* provides the history and social context for weaving, as well as practical guidelines for making tāniko. The clear and concise graphs and drawings can be used as a beginner's guide or a refresher resource, or simply to enjoy and admire this artform.

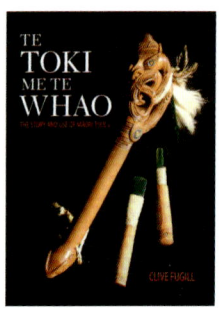

TE TOKI ME TE WHAO: THE STORY AND USE OF MĀORI TOOLS
Clive Fugill

978-0-947506-13-1
PB, 250 x 185 mm portrait, 152 pp, b&w with 8 pp colour

Te Toki me te Whao is a complete historical record as well as a practical guide to the use of Māori tools and technology. Written by an esteemed master carver, the book traces the mythical origins of wood carving and stone implements in the Pacific, the location and use of materials in Aotearoa, the manufacture of tools, and how to use them in making works of wood, stone and bone.

GREENSTONE CARVING: TECHNIQUES AND CONCEPTS IN POUNAMU
Len Gale

978-1-99-004216-4
PB, 250 x 185 portrait, 84 pp, colour

This concise guide to the art of greenstone carving takes readers from the origins of pounamu/greenstone through the basics of the artform: design, tools and techniques, different stone types and potential projects. Len Gale explains popular Māori designs such as hei tiki, toki, pekapeka, mere and patu alongside detailed drawings and photographs.

Available from good booksellers everywhere.
www.oratia.co.nz